ENGLISH PHRASAL VERBS
BOOK 1
3 WORDS A DAY

KEITH S. FOLSE

WAYZGOOSE PRESS

English Phrasal Verbs Book 1. 3 Words a Day.

Copyright © 2023 by Keith S. Folse

Edited by Kelly Sippell

Cover design by GetCovers.com

CONTENTS

LIST OF VERBS

PHRASAL VERBS IN BOOK 1 (BY LESSON)

Lesson 1: come back; go on; pick up

Lesson 2: come up; find out; go back

Lesson 3: come out; grow up; take on

Lesson 4: come in; go out; set up

Lesson 5: get back; give up; point out

Lesson 6: make up; sit down; turn out

Lesson 7: come on; end up; get out

Lesson 8: figure out; go down; look up

Lesson 9: come down; get up; take out

Lesson 10: show up; take off; work out

PHRASAL VERBS IN BOOK 1 (ALPHABETICAL)

come back (*first use*: Lesson 1), [*recycled in*: Lessons 5, 9]

come down (9)

come in (4)

come on (7), [6, 8]

come out (3), [5]

come up (2), [4]

end up (7), [8, 9, 10]

figure out (8), [10]

find out (2), [3, 5, 8]

get back (5), [6]

get out (7)

get up (9), [10]

give up (5), [8]

go back (2), [3, 7, 9]

go down (8)

go on (1), [2, 7, 9]

go out (4), [5, 9]

grow up (3), [4]

look up (8)

make up (6), [10]

pick up (1), [2, 7, 9]

point out (5), [7]

set up (4), [9]

show up (10)

sit down (6)

take off (10)

take on (3), [6]

take out (9)

turn out (6), [8]

work out (10)

INTRODUCTION

Phrasal verbs are one of the most difficult parts of English. They cause headaches for English learners no matter what your first language is. This book will help you with the phrasal verbs that are most frequent in spoken English.

To function well in a new language, you need vocabulary—and lots of it! Some studies say you can do simple things with just 1,000 words, but you can't really speak any language with just 1,000 words. Other experts have said you need 5,000 words, and some recent studies now say you need 10,000 (or even more!) words to speak your new language well. The more vocabulary you have in a new language, the better your speaking and listening will be.

A **phrasal verb** is one type of vocabulary. It consists of a verb and a preposition. The verb is usually a very simple short word like *get, make,* or *take.* The most common prepositions in phrasal verbs include *out, up, back down, in, over,* and *off* (Gardner and Davies, 2007).

The problem for English learners is that these two words together have **a new meaning that is not the same as the meaning of just the verb or the meaning of just the preposition**. If you know the meaning of the verb and the meaning of the preposition, it does not mean you know the meaning of the phrasal verb. The meanings are often very different.

For example, let's look at the phrasal verb *call off. Call* mostly means to contact someone on the phone, and *off* is the opposite of *on*. But *call off* means *cancel* and has no connection to a phone: *The coach called off the game.*

Learning phrasal verbs is very difficult. English has hundreds of phrasal verbs, and each phrasal verb can have several meanings.

WHY ARE THE 150 PHRASAL VERBS IN THIS BOOK IMPORTANT?

You can easily find a list of phrasal verbs on the internet, but those are just lists taken from big dictionaries. Many of those phrasal verbs are not so common, which makes them a waste of your time, and your time is important.

In these five books about phrasal verbs, you will practice the 150 most frequently used phrasal verbs in English. This list is the result of an extensive computer analysis of a large collection of approximately 130 million words of spoken English (PHaVE List: Garnier & Schmitt, 2015).

Sometimes one phrasal verb can have five or more meanings, so what should you learn first? You should learn the most common meanings, so the books in this series teach only the top meanings of each phrasal verb based on important information from a very detailed study by Liu & Myers (2020). The meanings are listed **in order of frequency**, so the first meaning is more frequently used than the second meaning, etc. (A few changes from the original list have been made for better learning.)

In sum, these books teach the most common phrasal verbs with the most common meanings in spoken English. Information about the 150 verbs chosen for these books comes from these sources:

Adolphs, Svenja, and Dawn Knight. "Building a spoken corpus." *The Routledge handbook of corpus linguistics (2010): 38–52.*

Davies, Mark. *The corpus of contemporary American English (COCA).* (2008 -): available online at https://www.english-corpora.org/coca/.

Gardner, Dee, and Mark Davies. "Pointing out frequent phrasal verbs: A corpus-based analysis." *TESOL Quarterly,* 41.2 (2007): 339–359.

Garnier, Mélodie, and Norbert Schmitt. "The PHaVE List: A pedagogical list of phrasal verbs and their most frequent meaning senses." *Language Teaching Research* 19.6 (2015): 645–666.

Garnier, Mélodie, and Norbert Schmitt. "Picking up polysemous phrasal verbs: How many do learners know and what facilitates this knowledge?" *System* 59 (2016): 29–44.

Liu, Dilin. "The most frequently used English phrasal verbs in American and British English: A multicorpus examination." *TESOL Quarterly* 45.4 (2011): 661–688.

Liu, Dilin, and Daniel Myers. "The most-common phrasal verbs with their key meanings for spoken and academic written English: A corpus analysis." *Language Teaching Research* 24.3 (2020): 403–424.

HOW ARE THESE BOOKS ORGANIZED?

There are five books in this series that cover phrasal verbs. The phrasal verbs in Book 1 are more common than those in Book 2, etc., so you should start with Book 1 and continue through the books in order: 2, 3, 4, 5. The order is based on an analysis of millions of words of real English.

Each book has 10 lessons. Each lesson has 3 phrasal verbs. That lesson will focus on those 3 phrasal verbs, but it will also review some of the phrasal verbs from earlier lessons, so you should also do the lessons in order.

Each lesson has these **6 practice activities**:

- **Activity 1**: CONVERSATION PRACTICE
- **Activity 2**: LEARNING NEW PHRASAL VERBS
- **Activity 3**: PRACTICING IMPORTANT PHRASES
- **Activity 4**: USING CORRECT PREPOSITIONS
- **Activity 5**: VERBS IN CONTEXT

- **Activity 6**: ONLINE PRACTICE (with a link allowing for 5 different kinds of online practice, including one for instruction)

PRACTICAL ADVICE FOR LEARNING VOCABULARY

You need a lot of vocabulary, and no one can learn this vocabulary for you. A good teacher and a good book can help, but in the end, it's all up to you.

To get more vocabulary, you need to read things in English that interest you. You need to practice speaking in English. You should try to find a conversation partner who can help you practice your lessons of three English phrasal verbs.

Keep a vocabulary notebook, either a traditional paper notebook or an electronic notebook. Every time you see a new English word, write it down. Ask yourself, "Is this word important for me in my English?" If the answer is yes, then ask, "How is this word used?" If the answer is no, then skip it and keep looking for another word.

To remember a new word, look at it carefully. Is there anything different or special about the word that can help you remember it? Is the spelling unusual or new to me? Is the word really long? Does it have any double letters?

Examples:

- VALLEY: You can remember the word *valley* because it begins with the letter V and a valley is shaped like the letter V.

- ENVELOPE: You can remember the word *envelope* because it starts with *e* and ends with *e*, and not many words in English start and end with the letter *e*.
- MUSTARD: A personal example is the word *mustard*. I like mustard a lot, so I know I need that word when I order a sandwich at a restaurant. If I don't know this word, then I should look for that word in a dictionary and then think of something to help me remember it. To do this well, I am going to imagine a big yellow **M** on top of my sandwich, representing mustard. Whenever you find a new word, try to find something that makes that word different or special to you personally.
- DOZEN: Every time you see a new word that you think is useful for your English purposes, you should stop and make a short example in your head. If the word is *dozen*, then say to yourself, "a dozen eggs, a dozen roses, a dozen cookies." It's okay to practice English with yourself in your own head. This is in fact very good practice. Use the new word and then talk to yourself (silently). It can be something as simple as "I would like some mustard, please." Yes, practice English with yourself by making a short example with each new word.

7 SUGGESTIONS FOR USING THIS BOOK

1. Open the book! Do the lessons! Many students buy a new book but do not complete the book. This book has only 10 lessons, and each lesson is short. Make time to read the book.

2. Do all the exercises. Even if an exercise seems easy, do it. The more times your brain "touches" each phrasal verb, the better your English vocabulary will become.

3. Each lesson teaches you only 3 phrasal verbs, but these verbs can have multiple meanings. In fact, many have two meanings, but others can have four or five. Everyone learns differently. Some people can do one lesson in one day, but most people will need a few days with each lesson to really learn the information. Only you know how much time you need for each lesson, so work hard and try to learn these very common, very useful phrasal verbs.

4. When you learn a new phrasal verb, try to learn a very short phrase with the verb. For example, when you learn FIND OUT, you should learn FIND OUT THE ANSWER or FIND OUT HER PHONE NUMBER. When you learn SET UP, you should try to remember SET UP AN APPOINTMENT or SET UP A MEETING.

5. Translations are very good when you first learn a new phrasal verb, but a translation is not your final goal. Your goal is to understand and use the phrasal verb. After you have a clear translation, then make sure you do step 3: Learn a short phrase with the verb.

6. Every time you see a new phrasal verb, immediately try to make a personal example in your head that is meaningful to you. For example, when you learn PICK UP, ask yourself, "How can I make an example with PICK UP about my life now?" Maybe you will say "I need to PICK UP my friend at the airport tonight" or "Please PICK UP the baby." Write it down. Say this example in your head. It is much better if you practice your new phrasal verb in your head before you try to use it in real conversation.

7. Try to use your new vocabulary in your conversations in English. If you have a conversation partner, share your list of 3 phrasal verbs from your lesson and tell your partner that the goal is to use these 3 phrasal verbs as much as possible in your conversation.

8. Do not worry about mistakes. Remember: Practice makes perfect, so practice, practice, practice!

Good luck learning lots of English vocabulary!

Keith S. Folse

LESSON 1

COME BACK; GO ON; PICK UP

ACTIVITY 1: CONVERSATION PRACTICE

Two coworkers are at work. Pam stops by Ryan's office.

Read this conversation. Think about the meanings of the **3 bold verbs**. Then answer the comprehension questions.

> **Pam**: Hi, Ryan, what's **going on**?
> **Ryan**: Not a lot. I'm just getting this presentation ready for tomorrow's meeting. The boss said it's going to be an important meeting.
> **Pam**: What's the meeting about?
> **Ryan**: We're trying to get this company to become a new client of ours. I really think we could help them with their advertising.
> **Pam**: Ok, I hope everything goes well. Hey, by the way, have you seen Andy?
> **Ryan**: No, but I'm supposed to see him in about 15 or 20 minutes. Why?
> **Pam**: Great. Can you do me a favor? Can you ask him to **pick up** the new contracts from the Human Resources office?
> **Ryan**: Yes, sure. I'll ask him to get those contracts.
> **Pam**: Oh, and when he **comes back**, ask him to bring all the contracts to me so I can sign them.
> **Ryan**: Yep, I'll do that.
> **Pam**: Thanks a lot.

1. What is Ryan doing?

    a. He is attending a meeting.
    b. He is preparing for a meeting.
    c. He is picking up a presentation.

2. When does Pam want to see Andy?

a. Before Ryan comes back from lunch.

b. After Pam signs the contracts.

c. When Andy comes back from picking up the papers.

3. What is Andy going to pick up?

a. contracts

b. presentations

c. advertising materials

4. Which adjective best describes this conversation between Pam and Ryan?

a. angry

b. friendly

c. surprising

5. What is Ryan's response to Pam's request?

a. He explains he is too busy.

b. He agrees to do it.

c. He suggests someone else.

6. While this conversation is going on, what is Andy doing?

a. He is making a presentation for a new client.

b. He is helping Ryan with tomorrow's presentation.

c. We don't know what Andy is doing.

∾

ACTIVITY 2: LEARNING NEW PHRASAL VERBS

Read this information about 3 phrasal verbs. Study the example sentences carefully. To help learn them, read the example sentences aloud or write them on a sheet of paper or in a document.

#1: COME BACK

1: return to a place; return to a topic in a conversation or discussion

- Let's first talk about what kind of car you want, and then we'll **come back** to the price.
- After my brother left his job in Germany, he **came back** to the U.S.

~

#2: GO ON

2A: happen

- What is **going on** here?
- When I walked into the room, I didn't know what was **going on**.

2B: continue (doing something)

- **Go on.** I want to hear how your story ends.
- It was raining, but the game **went on** anyway.

~

#3: PICK UP

3A: get something or someone from a place; collect something that fell

- I went to the store to **pick up** some bread and some cheese.
- My hands are full. Can you **pick up** that spoon for me?

3B: learn something new and special, often by chance and without effort

- Sarah **picked up** her accent when she lived in Ireland.
- Here is some advice I **picked up** from my grandpa.

3C: start again after a pause or break

- Unfortunately, our time today is up, but I hope we can **pick up** this discussion tomorrow.
- Good morning, class. Today we'll **pick up** our story with what happened in England immediately after the death of Queen Elizabeth II.

~

ACTIVITY 3: PRACTICING IMPORTANT PHRASES

Give the phrasal verb for the meaning. Be sure to use the correct verb tense.

1. return to a place = _____ _____ to a place
2. what is happening = what is _____ _____
3. start yesterday's discussion again = _____ _____ yesterday's discussion again
4. please, continue = please, _____ _____
5. learned a computer shortcut from a friend = _____ _____ a computer shortcut from a friend

∼

ACTIVITY 4: USING CORRECT PREPOSITIONS

Read the sentences carefully and add the missing prepositions for each phrasal verb.

1. Sarah **picked** _____ Spanish when she lived in Mexico.
2. This is a great story. **Go** _____. Please don't stop.
3. I hope we can **pick** _____ this discussion when we meet again tomorrow.
4. My brother worked in Germany for ten years and then **came** _____ home.
5. I went to the store to **pick** _____ some bread and some cheese.
6. What's **going** _____ here?

∼

ACTIVITY 5: VERBS IN CONTEXT

Use the context to select the correct verb for the sentence.

1. The clouds are very dark, but I think today's game will (come back, go on, pick up) anyway.
2. Oh, no! I dropped everything. Can you help me (come back, go on, pick up) all these coins?
3. I'm not sure what's going to (come back, go on, pick up) at the meeting tonight.
4. The cook (came back, went on, picked up) that idea when he was living in Mexico.
5. Class, yesterday we were talking about the Mayans in Guatemala, and today I'd like to (come back, go on, pick up) to this same topic.

∼

ACTIVITY 6: ONLINE PRACTICE

You can practice the phrasal verbs from this lesson at

https://tinyurl.com/3vfr9hry

Here you can use *Flashcards*, *Learn*, or *Match*. You can also have more guided practice with *Q-Chat*, which offers *Teach me*, *Quiz me*, and *Apply my knowledge*.

Answers for Lesson 1

Activity 1

1. b
2. c
3. a
4. b
5. b
6. c

Activity 3

1. come back
2. going on
3. pick up
4. go on
5. picked up

Activity 4

1. up
2. on
3. up
4. back
5. up
6. on

Activity 5

1. go on
2. pick up
3. go on
4. picked up
5. come back

LESSON 2
COME UP; FIND OUT; GO BACK

ACTIVITY 1: CONVERSATION PRACTICE

Two friends are talking about cars.

Read this conversation. Think about the meanings of the **3 new bold verbs**. Remember the meanings of the <u>underlined verbs</u> from earlier lessons. Then answer the comprehension questions.

Sam: Hey, what's <u>going on</u>?

Kevin: Oh, I'm looking at car websites.

Sam: Oh, really?

Kevin: Yes, I'm trying to **find out** the price of a new car.

Sam: Really? I didn't know you wanted to get a new car.

Kevin: Yeah, it's time.

Sam: Okay, but why now? You just moved here, and I know you must have some expenses with that kind of move.

Kevin: Well, the car I have is getting kind of old, so I think it's time for a new one. I've been looking at websites to <u>pick up</u> ideas for the kind of car I might get.

Sam: Have you seen anything you like?

Kevin: Yes, of course, and that's exactly the problem.

Sam: What do you mean?

Kevin: I see cars I like but, Sam, I don't think I can do this now.

Sam: Why not?

Kevin: The answer is simple. It's a topic that **comes up** a lot when I talk about getting a new car. It's money.

Sam: I understand the feeling. What if you **go back** to the place where you bought your current car? Do you think they might give you a better deal?

Kevin: Hmmm, maybe… Thanks, I guess that's a good idea.

1. What is Kevin looking at on the internet?

    a. car loans
    b. car repairs
    c. car prices

2. What does Kevin need to come up with?

    a. money
    b. a new car
    c. a different plan for Sam

3. What is Sam's suggestion for Kevin?

    a. Kevin should come up with the down payment as soon as possible.
    b. Kevin should use public transportation if his old car has any problems.
    c. Kevin should return to the place where he bought his current car.

4. Which of these statements is true?

    a. Sam told Kevin about a new place that sells cars.
    b. Kevin thinks his car is a little old.
    c. Kevin wants to buy an electric car this time.

5. How does Kevin feel about the suggestion that Sam came up with?

    a. He is grateful and thinks it's a good idea.
    b. He is annoyed and rejects the idea.
    c. He is confused and doesn't understand the idea.

6. What was Kevin's original plan to find out the information about the car?

    a. To ask Sam for help.
    b. To look at websites.
    c. To talk to a friend who owns a Toyota Corolla now.

∼

ACTIVITY 2: LEARNING NEW PHRASAL VERBS

Read this information about 3 phrasal verbs. Study the example sentences carefully. To help learn them, read the example sentences aloud or write them on a sheet of paper or in a document.

#4: COME UP

4A: happening very soon or suddenly

- Hey, don't forget that our family reunion is **coming up** in just a few weeks.
- The deadline to pay that bill is **coming up** really soon.

4B: COME UP WITH: create or produce

- If you can **come up with** a better idea, please let me know.
- Michael **came up with** the name for his new company by himself.

4C: COME UP TO: move very near

- Is your new cat friendly? Will she **come up to** me if I put out my hand?
- The police officer **came up to** our front door to ask us a few questions.

4D: occur or appear (especially used with a topic, a situation, or a problem)

- In your job interview tomorrow, don't ask about salary unless it **comes up**.
- No, in our talk yesterday, that topic never **came up**.

∽

#5: FIND OUT

5: receive or learn information for the first time

- How did you **find out** your flight was canceled?
- I just **found out** my sister and her family are coming to visit me next month.

~

#6: GO BACK (TO)

6: return to a place or return to doing an activity

- After lunch, I usually **go back** to the office.
- As soon as Jorge's leg was better, he **went back** to playing tennis every day.

~

ACTIVITY 3: PRACTICING IMPORTANT PHRASES

Give the phrasal verb for the meaning. Be sure to use the correct verb tense.

1. discover the answer to number 7 = _____ _____ the answer to number 7
2. create an idea = _____ _____ _____ an idea
3. return to a place = _____ _____ to a place
4. my birthday is happening soon = my birthday is

   _____ _____

5. return to doing an activity = _____ _____ to doing an activity

~

ACTIVITY 4: USING CORRECT PREPOSITIONS

Read the sentences carefully and add the missing prepositions for each phrasal verb.

1. How did you **find** _____ the price of a new Toyota Corolla?
2. When my elbow is better, I hope to be able to **go** _____ to playing golf.
3. I had an online meeting this morning, and now another one is **coming** _____ in half an hour.
4. We didn't know there was an earthquake there. How did you **find** _____?
5. I like your cat's name. How did you **come** _____ _____ it?

~

ACTIVITY 5: VERBS IN CONTEXT

Use the context to select the correct verb for the sentence.

1. Hey, your name (came up, came up to, found out, went back, went back to) yesterday when I was talking with my boss.
2. Do I need to remind you that my birthday is (coming up, coming up to, finding out, going back, going back to) soon?
3. As soon as my last class is over, I usually have to (come up, find out, go back) to work right away.

4. How did you (come up, come up to, find out, go back, go back to) that she has a dog?
5. As I was sitting on the bench, a cat (came up, came up to, found out, went back, went back to) me.

∽

ACTIVITY 6: ONLINE PRACTICE

You can practice the phrasal verbs from this lesson at

https://tinyurl.com/yfjjkd6a

Here you can use *Flashcards, Learn,* or *Match.* You can also have more guided practice with *Q-Chat,* which offers *Teach me, Quiz me,* and *Apply my knowledge.*

Answers for Lesson 2

Activity 1

1. c
2. a
3. c
4. b
5. a
6. b

Activity 3

1. find out
2. come up with
3. go back
4. coming up
5. go back

Activity 4

1. out
2. back
3. up
4. out
5. up with

Activity 5

1. came up
2. coming up
3. go back
4. find out
5. came up to

LESSON 3

COME OUT; GROW UP; TAKE ON

ACTIVITY 1: CONVERSATION PRACTICE

Two friends are talking about some good news.

Read this conversation. Think about the meanings of the **3 new bold verbs**. Remember the meanings of the <u>underlined verbs</u> from earlier lessons. Then answer the comprehension questions.

Olivia: Hey, I heard you might publish a book.

Nicole: Yes, that's right. I'm working on a book.

Olivia: Wow, that's great news. Congratulations! I didn't know you were a writer.

Nicole: I've actually always been interested in writing. I started working seriously on this book about two years ago. And now it's almost finished!

Olivia: So what's this book about?

Nicole: It's a story about a young woman and her first years away from home.

Olivia: Oh, that sounds interesting.

Nicole: The main character was born in Korea, but her family moved to Canada when she was only seven. She **grew up** in Vancouver, but later she moved to Montreal and got a new job in a new city where she didn't know anyone at all. She also decided to <u>go back</u> to school to finish college. This book is about how she deals with all these first-time things like being away from her family and having to get a new apartment and things like that. Pretty quickly, she realizes she has **taken on** too much in this new place and has to find a way to deal with all of it.

Olivia: Wow, I get it. That sounds like a really cool story.

Nicole: Thanks. It's still a work in progress, but I'm feeling good about it.

Olivia: So do you have any idea when this book might **come out**?

Nicole: Oh, it depends on a lot of things, but for now, I hope to finish the manuscript by the end of this month, so I'd say the book will probably be out in about six months from today. I still have a lot of work left to do, but it's going well.

Olivia: Well, congratulations, Nicole, on this great news. I'm really happy for you.

Nicole: Thanks, Olivia. When I <u>find out</u> the publication date, I'll let you know.

Olivia: Great.

1. Which represents the correct timeline of places?

   a. Korea, Vancouver, Montreal
   b. Korea, Montreal, Vancouver
   c. Canada, Korea, Montreal

2. How old is the main character in the book now?

   a. probably only 7 years old
   b. probably about 23 years old
   c. at least 50 years old

3. When might we first be able to buy Nicole's new book?

   a. next week
   b. in 6 months
   c. in about 2 years

4. How did Olivia find out that Nicole was writing a book?

    a. Nicole texted Olivia several weeks ago.
    b. Nicole and Olivia were together in the same writing club, so this book was never a secret.
    c. We don't know how Olivia found out.

5. What challenge does the main character in Nicole's story face?

    a. dealing with a family crisis in a new city
    b. writing her first book in a different language
    c. adjusting to life away from home

6. Which of these does Nicole hope to achieve by the end of the month?

    a. She hopes to finish her book manuscript.
    b. She hopes to start a new job in the same city.
    c. She hopes to find a bigger place to live.

~

ACTIVITY 2: LEARNING NEW PHRASAL VERBS

Read this information about 3 phrasal verbs. Study the example sentences carefully. To help learn them, read the example sentences aloud or write them on a sheet of paper or in a document.

#7: COME OUT

7A: announce publicly

- The mayor has **come out** against building a bigger jail in the downtown area.
- I think most people were surprised when the president **came out** in favor of free university education.

7B: physically leave or remove from a place

- The students usually **come out** of the building around 3:30.
- I've washed this shirt three times, but the ketchup stain won't **come out**.

7C: a new book, movie, or song is released

- When did the movie *Avengers Endgame* **come out**?
- I think that song **came out** in 2021.

~

#8: GROW UP

8: become older; become more mature

- Children who **grow up** in a family where the parents speak two languages are lucky.
- I was born in Saudi Arabia, but I **grew up** in Morocco.

∾

#9: TAKE ON

9A: accept or agree to do something, especially something that is challenging or difficult

- When she became a manager, she had to **take on** a lot of new duties.
- He **took on** too much extra work and got sick.

9B: play against in a game

- It is exciting when all these really good athletes **take on** each other in the Olympics.
- Argentina **took on** France in the final match of the World Cup in 2022.

∾

ACTIVITY 3: PRACTICING IMPORTANT PHRASES

Give the phrasal verb for the meaning. Be sure to use the correct verb tense.

1. a new movie was released = a new movie _____ _____
2. become older = _____ _____
3. speak in public in favor of a new plan = _____ _____ in favor of a new plan
4. he lived most of life in Los Angeles = he _____ _____ in Los Angeles

5. begin to work on a challenge = _____ _____ a challenge

~

ACTIVITY 4: USING CORRECT PREPOSITIONS

Read the sentences carefully and add the missing prepositions for each phrasal verb.

1. Oh, no! I got ink on my new jeans, and an ink stain will never **come** _____.
2. When the movie *Barbie* **came** _____ in 2023, it broke all kinds of sales records.
3. Okay, I know you were born in Colombia, but where did you **grow** _____?
4. Next month I'm going to **take** _____ five new clients.
5. If your candidate **comes** _____ against higher pay for teachers, will you still support her?
6. In the Women's World Cup Final in 2023, England **took** _____ Spain, and Spain was the winner 1-0.

~

ACTIVITY 5: VERBS IN CONTEXT

Use the context to select the correct verb for the sentence.

1. You never want to accept responsibility for anything. You need to (come out, grow up, take on).

2. Has any political party (come out, grow up, take on) in favor of increasing the driving age?

3. I'm afraid I've (come out, grown up, taken on) too much work. Can you help me?

4. I was only seven years old when the movie *E.T. the Extra Terrestrial* (came out, grew up, took on).

5. If you (come out, grow up, take on) in a certain place, of course you will probably speak with an accent from that area.

~

ACTIVITY 6: ONLINE PRACTICE

You can practice the phrasal verbs from this lesson at

https://tinyurl.com/22mnfpdf

Here you can use *Flashcards*, *Learn*, or *Match*. You can also have more guided practice with *Q-Chat*, which offers *Teach me*, *Quiz me*, and *Apply my knowledge*.

Answers for Lesson 3

Activity 1

1. a
2. b
3. b
4. c
5. c
6. a

Activity 3

1. came out
2. grow up
3. come out
4. grew up
5. take on

Activity 4

1. out
2. out
3. up
4. on
5. out
6. on

Activity 5

1. grow up
2. come out
3. taken on
4. came out
5. grow up

LESSON 4

COME IN; GO OUT; SET UP

ACTIVITY 1: CONVERSATION PRACTICE

Two friends who haven't seen each other in a while meet again.

Read this conversation. Think about the meanings of the **3 new bold verbs**. Remember the meanings of the <u>underlined verbs</u> from earlier lessons. Then answer the comprehension questions.

Emily: Daniel! Oh, no! What happened to you?

Daniel: Oh, I guess you didn't hear about my surgery. I had shoulder surgery about a month ago.

Emily: No, I didn't know that. Are you okay?

Daniel: Well, yes, it's getting better. The doctor wants me to **come in** again next week, but he said I'm making good progress.

Emily: Gosh, your arm is in a sling. It looks bad. Are you in any pain?

Daniel: Thanks for the concern, but no, I'm not in any pain. I just want to be able to **go out** with my friends, but I can't do that for a little while longer. And, Emily, I really miss playing basketball with them on the weekends. You know, I <u>grew up</u> playing basketball all the time, and I really miss it.

Emily: I'm sure you'll play again one day. Can you work now?

Daniel: Well, luckily, the problem is with my left shoulder, and I'm right-handed, so I can still do a lot of things, but I only have one hand for the time being.

Emily: And I guess that must be hard.

Daniel: It's not too bad. I'm working, but my boss at the bank is letting me work from home, so that helps.

Emily: And you can get all your work done?

Daniel: Well, I had to get someone to help me **set up** the workspace in my office a little differently, and so now things are easier for me to access. I mean, I can type, and that's the most important thing for me to be able to do my work. I can do a lot of things, but I'm still limited.

Emily: That sounds tough. Really tough. Listen, Daniel, if you need me to do anything, if any kind of problem comes up, just let me know, okay?

Daniel: Emily, thank you. You're a really good friend, but I think I've taken care of most things already.

Emily: Okay, great, but if you change your mind at any time, please just let know.

1. Which of Daniel's shoulders was operated on?

    a. Daniel's left shoulder
    b. Daniel's right shoulder
    c. both of Daniel's shoulders

2. How much pain does Daniel feel now?

    a. none
    b. some
    c. a lot

3. Which is true about Daniel and work now?

    a. He can't work for one more month.
    b. He's working from home.
    c. He's already back in the office.

4. How do Emily and Daniel know each other?

a. They work together.

b. They have the same doctor.

c. We don't know from this story.

5. What does Daniel do for a living?

a. He works at home.

b. He works at a bank.

c. We don't know from this story.

6. Which of these is true from the information here?

a. Daniel goes out with Emily.

b. Daniel and Emily grew up together.

c. Daniel appreciates Emily's friendship.

~

ACTIVITY 2: LEARNING NEW PHRASAL VERBS

Read this information about 3 phrasal verbs. Study the example sentences carefully. To help learn them, read the example sentences aloud or write them on a sheet of paper or in a document.

#10: COME IN

10A: enter an area or a place

- Our boss has asked everyone who works from home to **come in** next week.

- The window was open, and a small bird **came in** the room.

10B: enter a situation or a space

- Sometimes when a new boss **comes in**, there are a lot of big changes.
- A few years ago, a big supermarket **came in** and, as a result, many of the small shops in the area closed.

～

#11: GO OUT

11A: date someone

- Are Melissa and Joe **going out**?
- They **went out** with each other for three years before they got married.

11B: **GO OUT (OF):** leave a place or situation

- Once you enter the concert, you can't **go out** and come back in.
- I think baggy jeans were popular in the 1990s, but they **went out of** style in the 2000s.

～

#12: SET UP

12A: create or organize something (like a meeting or a schedule)

- My boss wants to **set up** an online meeting for next Tuesday.
- Do you know how to **set up** a monthly bank payment?

12B: build or install something concrete, like a business

- It took Sam a long time to **set up** his office furniture just like he likes it.
- This company says it can teach you how to **set up** a website in seven simple steps.

∼

ACTIVITY 3: PRACTICING IMPORTANT PHRASES

Give the phrasal verb for the meaning. Be sure to use the correct verb tense.

1. go on a date with Maria = _____ _____ with Maria
2. created a schedule = _____ _____ a schedule
3. organized a new group = _____ _____ a new group
4. left the building = _____ _____ of the building
5. no one entered this room = no one _____ _____ this room

~

ACTIVITY 4: USING CORRECT PREPOSITIONS

Read the sentences carefully and add the missing prepositions for each phrasal verb.

1. How long have Megan and Chance been **going** _____
   with each other?
2. A new detective **came** _____ and solved the murder
   in just a week.
3. Sue, would you please close the door when you **go**
   _____?
4. How much would it cost to **set** _____ a simple
   website for my business?
5. I knocked on the door and heard a voice say "**Come**
   _____," so I did.
6. To **set** _____ a bank account, you'll need an ID and at
   least $25.

~

ACTIVITY 5: VERBS IN CONTEXT

Use the context to select the correct verb for the sentence.

1. Do you need help (coming in, going out, setting up)
   your account and password?
2. Can you help me (come in, go out, set up) the GPS in
   my new car?

3. We didn't know Emma and Ethan were a couple. How long have they been (coming in, going out, setting up)?

4. Melissa usually (comes in, goes out, sets up) for a walk about an hour before sunset.

5. After the old director left and the new director (came in, set up, went out) in 2021, the employees were happier because of the new leadership.

∽

ACTIVITY 6: ONLINE PRACTICE

You can practice the phrasal verbs from this lesson at

https://tinyurl.com/dpvbyhaa

Here you can use *Flashcards*, *Learn*, or *Match*. You can also have more guided practice with *Q-Chat*, which offers *Teach me*, *Quiz me*, and *Apply my knowledge*.

Answers for Lesson 4

Activity 1

1. a
2. a
3. b
4. c
5. b
6. c

Activity 3

1. go out
2. set up
3. set up
4. went out
5. came in

Activity 4

1. out
2. in
3. out
4. up
5. in
6. up

Activity 5

1. setting up
2. set up
3. going out
4. goes out
5. came in

LESSON 5

GET BACK; GIVE UP; POINT OUT

ACTIVITY 1: CONVERSATION PRACTICE

Two friends are talking about an upcoming surprise.

Read this conversation. Think about the meanings of the **3 new bold verbs**. Remember the meanings of the <u>underlined verbs</u> from earlier lessons. Then answer the comprehension questions.

Maria: Hey, guess what I'm going to get next week!

Jessica: I don't know. I **give up**.

Maria: A dog.

Jessica: What? A dog? Really?

Maria: Why not? Why are you so surprised?

Jessica: Wait, you're really serious? Do I really have to **point out** all the reasons to you? Gosh, Maria, I think the reasons are pretty obvious.

Maria: What do you mean?

Jessica: Well, for starters, you travel for work a lot. At least once a week, sometimes twice a week. And dogs like to <u>go out</u> for walks. You just can't keep a dog inside your tiny apartment without letting it go out every day. What are you going to do when you travel? Who's going to walk the dog?

Maria: Gee, you're right. That's a good point, I guess. I mean, I hadn't even thought about that."

Jessica: And Maria, let's be honest for a minute. You like things to be really clean, and that's cool, but what's going to happen when you <u>come back</u> home from one of your trips and <u>find out</u> the dog peed on your carpet? I know you. It's not the dog's fault, but you're not going to like it when the stain and the smell won't <u>come out</u> of the carpet.

Maria: Okay, you've made your point. I guess I need to

think about this idea a little more, but I sure would like to have a dog.

Jessica: All right. I understand. Hey, I need to **get back** home, so I'm leaving. Let me know what you decide to do about the dog, okay?

1. What does Maria do once or twice a week?

    a. She takes her dog to a special park.
    b. She goes out of town.
    c. She points out some problems to Jessica.

2. What is one problem with Maria's apartment?

    a. There is not enough space.
    b. Maria's roommate doesn't like dogs.
    c. The floors are made of wood.

3. Why does Maria want to get a pet?

    a. Because she travels a lot.
    b. Because Jessica suggests this idea.
    c. We don't know from this conversation.

4. Which of these statements is true?

    a. Maria likes everything to be very clean.
    b. Jessica thinks Maria should get a dog soon.
    c. Maria and Jessica will probably never talk to each other again.

5. How does Maria react to Jessica's comments about getting a dog?

    a. Maria and Jessica will choose a name for her
new dog.
    b. Maria wants to think about everything some more.
    c. Maria wants to set up a second meeting with Jessica.

6. How does Jessica end the conversation?

    a. She suggests that Maria should buy a smaller dog.
    b. She offers to help if Maria finds out how much a
new dog costs.
    c. She wants to know what Maria is going to do.

~

ACTIVITY 2: LEARNING NEW PHRASAL VERBS

Read this information about 3 phrasal verbs. Study the example sentences carefully. To help learn them, read the example sentences aloud or write them onto a sheet of paper or into a document.

#13: GET BACK (TO)

13: return to a place or activity

- What time did you **get back** last night?
- My vacation is over, and tomorrow I have to **get back** to the real world.

~

#14: GIVE UP

14A: stop having or doing something

- It's good manners to **give up** your seat on the bus or subway to an older person.
- When he hurt his leg, he had to **give up** his dream of winning an Olympic medal.

14B: surrender; quit an action

- A lot of people start a diet, but most **give up** after a few weeks.
- After almost a year of looking for a job in China, Marsha **gave up** and took a job here.

~

#15: POINT OUT

15: indicate or call attention to; comment about

- Good teachers **point out** the most important information for their students.
- The cashier **pointed out** that the shirt was missing two buttons, so I didn't buy it.

~

ACTIVITY 3: PRACTICING IMPORTANT PHRASES

Give the phrasal verb for the meaning. Be sure to use the correct verb tense.

1. stop playing video games = _____ _____ playing video games
2. return home = _____ _____ home
3. show a problem to someone = _____ _____ a problem to someone
4. quit = _____ _____
5. start studying German again = _____ _____ to studying German

∽

ACTIVITY 4: USING CORRECT PREPOSITIONS

Read the sentences carefully and add the missing prepositions for each phrasal verb.

1. What time do you usually **get** _____ from your lunch break?
2. My cousin got tired of looking for a job and finally just **gave** _____.
3. I want to **get** _____ in time to watch the baseball game on TV later.
4. My mom **pointed** _____ that I was going to be late for work, so I hurried up.
5. The doctor told me to **give** _____ fried foods, and that was hard to do.

6. Can you **point** _____ the best way to go from here to the hospital?

～

ACTIVITY 5: VERBS IN CONTEXT

Use the context to select the correct verb for the sentence.

1. Our guide (gave up, got back, pointed out) so many cool things on our free walking tour in central London.
2. Unfortunately, we missed our return flight from Brazil, so we (gave up, got back, pointed out) one day later than expected.
3. Today's puzzle is too hard. I don't know the answer. I tried for ten minutes and then just (got back, gave up, pointed out).
4. Learning English is tough, but I am not going to (get back, give up, point out).
5. My teacher (gave up, got back, pointed out) several spelling errors in my first paragraph.

～

ACTIVITY 6: ONLINE PRACTICES

You can practice the phrasal verbs from this lesson at

https://tinyurl.com/38uyyvyr

Here you can use *Flashcards*, *Learn*, or *Match*. You can also have more guided practice with *Q-Chat*, which offers *Teach me*, *Quiz me*, and *Apply my knowledge*.

Activity 5

1. pointed out
2. got back
3. gave up
4. give up
5. pointed out

LESSON 6

MAKE UP; SIT DOWN; TURN OUT

ACTIVITY 1: CONVERSATION PRACTICE

Two coworkers are talking about a trip.

Read this conversation. Think about the meanings of the **3 new bold verbs**. Remember the meanings of the underlined verbs from earlier lessons. Then answer the comprehension questions.

Ashley: Hey, Oscar. Good to see you. Welcome back!

Oscar: Thanks. It's good to be back.

Ashley: You were in Japan, right? How was it?

Oscar: Yes, I was there for about 10 days.

Ashley: That's so cool. So, when did you get back?

Oscar: Just last night. It was kind of late, almost midnight.

Ashley: That's late. You must be really tired.

Oscar: Well, yes, a little. I think it'll hit me later today when I start to get sleepy.

Ashley: Hey, did everything go okay with your flight?

Oscar: Well, to tell you the truth, I was dreading it, but it all **turned out** okay.

Ashley: So, you had no problems?

Oscar: Well, we had a delay of about 45 minutes before we left Tokyo, but the pilot said we'd be able to **make up for** this delay because we had such good flying conditions, and he was right because we actually landed in New York 15 minutes ahead of schedule.

Ashley: Well, that's good.

Oscar: And what was extra good was that I had a whole row to myself!

Ashley: Really? A whole row to yourself?

Oscar: Yes, I had the window seat and as soon as I **sat down**, I started looking around me to see if there might be some empty seats. They closed the door of the plane, and there was still no one next to me, so I had the whole row—all three seats—to myself.

Ashley: That's amazing—a whole row to yourself across the Pacific. And how long was the flight?

Oscar: It was supposed to be 14 hours and 15 minutes, but we actually arrived a little early, so I guess it was just under 14 hours.

Ashley: 14 hours? That's still such a long time. You know, I've never been on a super long flight like that. What do people do?

Oscar: Some people read, some watch movies or listen to music, and a lot of people just sleep. I watched two movies and slept a lot.

Ashley: Well, I'm glad you're back here now, and I hope you're feeling okay.

Oscar: Yes, I'm good.

Ashley: Okay, then let's talk about a big presentation you and I have to do in two weeks.

Oscar: What are you talking about?

Ashley: Well, while you were in Japan, we <u>took on</u> a new client, and you and I are in charge of <u>coming up with</u> a sales plan for their new product.

Oscar: <u>Come on,</u> then! Let's get started.

1. How long was Oscar away from the office?

   a. 10 days
   b. 14 days
   c. 15 days

2. When did Oscar arrive back in New York?

    a. yesterday morning

    b. yesterday afternoon

    c. last night

3. What did Oscar do during the flight to pass the time?

    a. He watched some movies and slept.

    b. He worked on a presentation about Japan.

    c. He read a book.

4. What part of the flight from Japan was Oscar really happy about?

    a. landing 15 minutes early

    b. having no one sitting next to him

    c. watching a really good movie

5. How long is the flight from Tokyo to New York normally?

    a. just under 14 hours

    b. 14 hours

    c. just over 14 hours

6. At the end of their meeting, what does Ashley suggest?

    a. She and Oscar should start doing some work.

    b. She and Oscar should have lunch together soon.

    c. Oscar should show her photos of his amazing trip.

$\approx$

ACTIVITY 2: LEARNING NEW PHRASAL VERBS

Read this information about 3 phrasal verbs. Study the example sentences carefully. To help learn them, read the example sentences aloud or write them on a sheet of paper or in a document.

#16: MAKE UP

16A: create or invent

- He decided to **make up** a story about losing his keys to explain why he was late again.
- I couldn't admit I overslept again, so I **made up** an excuse for being late.

16B: BE MADE UP OF: be part of something bigger

- The United States is **made up of** 50 states.
- The color green is **made up of** the colors blue and yellow.

16C: MAKE UP FOR: do something to fix something else; compensate

- I'd like to buy you dinner to **make up for** my bad behavior.
- She baked a cake for me to **make up for** forgetting my birthday.

16D: decide

- Some people take a long time to **make up** their mind.
- Once Mike **made up** his mind about which job to take, he felt a lot better.

∿

#17: SIT DOWN

17: move from a standing position to being on a chair, sofa, or similar

- This chair is for you. Please **sit down**.
- The teacher asked everyone to **sit down** so she could begin the class.

∿

#18: TURN OUT

18: proved to be true; become a certain way in the end

- How did everything with your presentation **turn out** yesterday?
- My weather app said it was going to rain, but today **turned out** to be a beautiful day.

∿

ACTIVITY 3: PRACTICING MPORTANT PHRASES

Give the phrasal verb for the meaning. Be sure to use the correct verb tense.

1. decide = _____ _____ your mind
2. everything proved to be fine = everything _____ _____ fine
3. move to a chair = _____ _____ in this chair
4. create a story = _____ _____ a story
5. your first cake was great in the end = your first cake _____ _____ great in the end

~

ACTIVITY 4: USING CORRECT PREPOSITIONS

Read the sentences carefully and add the missing prepositions for each phrasal verb.

1. She was nervous, but her presentation **turned** _____ fine.
2. Please **sit** _____ here.
3. Water is **made** _____ _____ hydrogen and oxygen.
4. We need you to **make** _____ your mind about the paint color for the walls.
5. How did your daughter's graduation **turn** _____?
6. The speaker asked everyone to **sit** _____.

~

ACTIVITY 5: VERBS IN CONTEXT

Use the context to select the correct verb for the sentence.

1. I am tired. Can you please (make up, make up of, make up for, sit down, turn out) an excuse for us so we don't have to go to the dinner tonight?
2. I know you're worried about your test, but I'm sure everything will (make up, make up of, make up for, sit down, turn out) great.
3. The doctor asked me to (make up, make up of, make up for, sit down, turn out) so he and I could talk about my test results.
4. We were worried about taking the bus to school every day, but it (made up, made up of, made up for, sat down, turned out) to be easy to do.
5. Canada is (made up, made up of, made up for, sat down, turned out) 10 provinces and 3 territories.

∾

ACTIVITY 6: ONLINE PRACTICE

You can practice the phrasal verbs from this lesson at

https://tinyurl.com/2s3p5mw2

Here you can use *Flashcards*, *Learn*, or *Match*. You can also have more guided practice with *Q-Chat*, which offers *Teach me*, *Quiz me*, and *Apply my knowledge*.

Answers for Lesson 6

Activity 1

1. a
2. c
3. a
4. b
5. c
6. a

Activity 3

1. make up
2. turned out
3. sit down
4. make up
5. turned out

Activity 4

1. out
2. down
3. up of
4. up
5. out
6. down

Activity 5

1. make up
2. turn out
3. sit down
4. turned out
5. made up of

LESSON 7

COME ON; END UP; GET OUT

ACTIVITY 1: CONVERSATION PRACTICE

Amanda calls her friend Melissa to see if she wants to go do something.

Read this conversation. Think about the meanings of the **3 new bold verbs.** Remember the meanings of the <u>underlined verbs</u> from earlier lessons. Then answer the comprehension questions.

Melissa: Hey, Amanda.

Amanda: Hey there! What are you up to?

Melissa: Not too much. I'm doing some laundry. What's <u>going on</u>?

Amanda: Well, I'm here at home, and it's a beautiful day. I don't think anyone should be inside today, and so I was wondering if you wanted to **get out** for a while.

Melissa: Oh, Amanda, thanks, but I don't know. I really want to finish the laundry. I don't have any time to do laundry during the week, so it's got to be today.

Amanda: By the way, let me <u>point out</u> that it's a really beautiful today, and you and I haven't seen each other in more than a month. **Come on**, Melissa. Let's go do something.

Melissa: I don't know.

Amanda: Look, there's a new ice cream shop near the park. It just opened last week, and I've heard they have some cool flavors. Let's go get some ice cream and talk for a while. Whenever you need to <u>go back</u> home, just let me know and I'll take you home, but you need to **get out of** the house today and enjoy this great weather.

Melissa: Okay, you win, but I have to finish this laundry first.

Amanda: So, when do you think you can go?

Melissa: So, let's see. Well, it's 1:00 now, so I think I can be free by 3:30 or 4:00 at the latest.
Amanda: Okay, how about if I <u>pick</u> you <u>up</u> at your place at 4:00?
Melissa: Yep, that sounds great. And if I **end up** finishing earlier, I'll call and let you know, but I think I need at least two hours to finish.
Amanda: Sure, that's sounds great. See you then.

1. What was Melissa doing when she called Amanda?

    a. Talking with her friend.
    b. Walking her dog.
    c. Doing something at home.

2. How does Melissa initially respond to Amanda's suggestion?

    a. She says she can't go out.
    b. She points out there is a new ice cream shop.
    c. She sets up another activity for them to do.

3. Which of these statements is true about Amanda?

    a. Amanda will pay for the ice cream for both of them.
    b. Amanda promises to do Melissa's laundry.
    c. Amanda offers to pick Melissa up.

4. What is the shortest amount of time Melissa thinks she needs before she can go out?

a. one hour
b. two hours
c. three hours

5. Why does Melissa think today is a good day for them go out?

a. Because it's Saturday.
b. Because the weather is so good.
c. Because Amanda needs to do the laundry.

6. How are Amanda and Melissa going to get to the ice cream shop?

a. They're walking together.
b. They're going in Amanda's car.
c. We don't know.

~

ACTIVITY 2: LEARNING NEW PHRASAL VERBS

Read this information about 3 phrasal verbs. Study the example sentences carefully. To help learn them, read the example sentences aloud or write them on a sheet of paper or in a document.

#19: COME ON

19A: a phrase that means to try harder or to keep doing what you're doing

- **Come on**, team! We can do this!
- **Come on**, Joe, we'll be late if you don't hurry up.

19B: showing disbelief, disagreement, or anger

- **Come on**. That story can't be true.
- **Come on**. You don't have to treat people like that.

~

#20: END UP

20: unexpectedly doing something that was not your original plan

- Our plan is to walk to the store, but we might **end up** driving if it starts to rain.
- I didn't want to visit my uncle today, but somehow, I **ended up** at his house anyway.

~

#21: GET OUT (OF)

21A: leave a place, especially one where you do not want to be

- We stay at home too much. We need to **get out** more.
- He was happy when he finally **got out of** jail.

21B: **GET OUT OF:** leave an unpleasant task or situation

- When I was a kid, I always tried to **get out of** going to school.
- Josh is trying to **get out of** our agreement now.

∾

ACTIVITY 3: PRACTICING IMPORTANT PHRASES

Give the phrasal verb for the meaning. Be sure to use the correct verb tense.

1. leave your car = _____ _____ of your car
2. we changed our mind and in the end ate tacos = we _____ _____ eating tacos
3. Try harder, guys! = _____ _____, guys!
4. we went to the store (but that was not our plan) = we _____ _____ going to the store
5. we were able to leave our meeting = we _____ _____ _____ our meeting

∾

ACTIVITY 4: USING CORRECT PREPOSITIONS

Read the sentences carefully and add the missing prepositions for each phrasal verb.

1. After a meeting with our lawyer, we were able to **get** _____ _____ our contract for that new car.

2. John, **come** _____, you can't say those kinds of things.
3. It was raining really hard, so we **ended** _____ staying home.
4. I know you're tired of hearing this, but **come** _____, she's our friend and we need to support her.
5. If you guys **end** _____ going to see a movie, let me know and I might go with you.
6. My little sister told me to **get** _____ of her room.

∿

ACTIVITY 5: VERBS IN CONTEXT

Use the context to select the correct verb for the sentence.

1. We need to (come on, end up, get out, get out of) the car here.
2. (Come on, End up, Get out, Get out of), we can't go to that party. We weren't invited.
3. At first, we didn't want to eat at a sushi restaurant, but we (came on, ended up, got out, got out of) going there because it was the closest place and we were so hungry. It was great!
4. A lot of people are trying to (come on, end up, get out, get out of) this area before the bad weather gets here.
5. How did you (come on, end up, get out, get out of) going to Honduras last month? I thought you told me you couldn't go. And where in Honduras were you? Tell me everything!

~

ACTIVITY 6: ONLINE PRACTICES

You can practice the phrasal verbs from this lesson at

https://tinyurl.com/2utuyx2a

Here you can use *Flashcards*, *Learn*, or *Match*. You can also have more guided practice with *Q-Chat*, which offers *Teach me*, *Quiz me*, and *Apply my knowledge*.

Answers for Lesson 7

Activity 1

1. c
2. a
3. a
4. b
5. b
6. b

Activity 3

1. get out
2. ended up
3. come on
4. ended up
5. got out of

Activity 4

1. out of
2. on
3. up
4. on
5. up
6. out

Activity 5

1. get out of
2. come on
3. ended up
4. get out of
5. end up

LESSON 8

FIGURE OUT; GO DOWN; LOOK UP

ACTIVITY 1: CONVERSATION PRACTICE

A husband and wife are talking about plans for their upcoming vacation.

Read this conversation. Think about the meanings of the **3 new bold verbs**. Remember the meanings of the <u>underlined verbs</u> from earlier lessons. Then answer the comprehension questions.

Michael: Hey, Sarah, how's everything going with our trip to Spain?

Sarah: Everything is fine. You know I've been looking at prices, and I have some great news that you're going to like.

Michael: Great! What did you <u>find out</u>?

Sarah: Okay, so we need to book two tickets to get there, plus our hotel for five nights, right?

Michael: Um… Is it five nights? Or six?

Sarah: No, it's just five. We leave here on the 10th and then come back on the 16th.

Michael: Isn't that six nights? Doesn't 16 minus 10 equal six? So we need six nights.

Sarah: No, actually it's only five. See, to **figure out** the number of hotel nights we need, you have to remember that even though we leave there on the 10th, we don't arrive in Spain until the next day, so the first day we need a hotel in Spain is the 11th. We're really only there from the 11th until the 16th. Our flight on the 10th is an overnight flight. Does that make sense?

Michael: Ha, yes! You are 100% right, and this is precisely why I prefer that you to make all these travel arrangements. Sarah, you're just really good with all these details.

Sarah: Thanks.

Michael: So, what's the good news?

Sarah: I **looked up** the price of our air tickets and the hotel. The air tickets were $1,200 each, and the hotel was around $600.

Michael: For a total of $3,000 then? 1200 and 1200 and 600 are 3,000.

Sarah: Yes, that's right, but then I <u>found out</u> from my friend Kayla that if we buy a travel package, we can…

Michael: Wait, a travel package? What does that mean?

Sarah: Well, some travel sites will sell you air and hotel together, and sometimes this travel package is cheaper than buying things separately.

Michael: <u>Come on,</u> really? So, we might <u>end up</u> saving some money?

Sarah: Yes, in our case, if we book the package, the total price **goes down** by $400.

Michael: So just $2,600 instead of $3,000?

Sarah: Yes, that's exactly right. A package deal <u>turns out</u> to be a better deal.

Michael: Okay, then, let's book that package deal right now.

Sarah: Great… because I've already done it. I couldn't <u>give up</u> a chance to save that much money. Everything is booked, and we <u>ended up</u> saving a lot of money.

1. What ended up happening with their new travel plans?

   a. Sarah and Michael ended up saving $400.
   b. Michael accidentally booked an extra hotel night.
   c. Sarah gave up their chance to travel to Spain.

2. Why did Michael think they needed six nights in a hotel?

    a. A friend of Michael's told him that a week in Spain is too long.
    b. Sarah made a mistake and told him they needed six nights.
    c. Michael forgot that the first night is on the plane.

3. What was the original cost of the air tickets for two people?

    a. $1,200
    b. $2,400
    c. $2,600

4. How did Sarah find out about a package deal?

    a. Michael told her.
    b. Kayla told her.
    c. Sarah has known about travel packages for a long time.

5. On which of these days will they not be in Spain?

    a. the 10th
    b. the 11th
    c. the 16th

6. What was Michael's response when he learned about the final price of their trip to Spain?

a. He was a little sad.
b. He was very angry.
c. He was happy.

∾

ACTIVITY 2: LEARNING NEW PHRASAL VERBS

Read this information about 3 phrasal verbs. Study the example sentences carefully. To help learn them, read the example sentences aloud or write them on a sheet of paper or in a document.

#22: FIGURE OUT

22: discover; solve; calculate

- Can you **figure out** what the answer to this math problem is?
- The police have finally **figured out** how the robbers were able to steal so much money.

∾

#23: GO DOWN

23A: move to a lower position

- Luckily, he didn't fall **going down** the stairs.
- If you just **go down** the list, you'll see many names you recognize.

23B: decrease in numerical value

- Everyone hopes the price of gasoline **goes down** soon.
- When the price of a ticket to Miami **went down**, I booked it right away.

∼

#24: LOOK UP

24A: look to the ceiling or the sky

- Please keep your eyes on your own test. Do not **look up** at me.
- If you **look up** now, you can see not one but three airplanes in the sky.

24B: **LOOK UP TO**: respect or admire someone as a role model

- Most kids **look up to** their heroes.
- I've always **looked up to** my mom because she had a hard life growing up.

24C: consult a book, a website, or a person for information

- You should **look up** words you don't know and then write them down.
- We usually just search the internet to **look up** the prices of the products we need.

ACTIVITY 3: PRACTICING IMPORTANT PHRASES

Give the phrasal verb for the meaning. Be sure to use the correct verb tense.

1. find the meaning of a phrasal verb in a dictionary = _____ _____ the meaning in a dictionary
2. the price of the ticket decreased = the price of the ticket _____ _____
3. discover the answer without any help = _____ _____ the answer without any help
4. move to a lower position on the stairs = _____ _____ the stairs
5. use the internet to find the exact location of the bank = use the internet to _____ _____ the exact location of the bank

ACTIVITY 4: USING CORRECT PREPOSITIONS

Read the sentences carefully and add the missing prepositions for each phrasal verb.

1. A friend told me about that new restaurant, so I decided to **look** _____ their menu online.
2. The first thing my dad does every day is try to **figure** _____ the answer to a word puzzle he plays.

3. I like sitting in front of a fireplace. When the flames start to **go** _____, you have to put on another log.
4. Is this elevator **going** _____ to the lobby?
5. Kids need to **look** _____ _____ the good adults around them. They need role models.
6. Can you listen to mom's message? I can't **figure** _____ what she's saying.

∾

ACTIVITY 5: VERBS IN CONTEXT

Use the context to select the correct verb for the sentence.

1. When we were camping last week, every night we were able to (figure out, go down, look up, look up to) and see many stars.
2. Did you hear the weather forecast? The temperature tonight is going to (figure out, go down, look up) to 10 degrees.
3. My boss is hard to read. I can't (figure out, go down, look up, look up to) if he really likes my work or not.
4. Our Spanish teacher lets us use an online dictionary in class to (figure out, go down, look up, look up to) words we don't know.
5. The police are still trying to (figure out, go down, look up, look up to) what happened.

∾

ACTIVITY 6: ONLINE PRACTICE

You can practice the phrasal verbs from this lesson at

https://tinyurl.com/ynecjn4j

Here you can use *Flashcards*, *Learn*, or *Match*. You can also have more guided practice with *Q-Chat*, which offers *Teach me*, *Quiz me*, and *Apply my knowledge*.

Answers for Lesson 8

Activity 1

1. a
2. c
3. b
4. b
5. a
6. c

Activity 3

1. look up
2. went down
3. figure out
4. go down
5. look up

Activity 4

1. up
2. out
3. down
4. down
5. up to
6. out

Activity 5

1. look up
2. go down
3. figure out
4. look up
5. figure out

LESSON 9

COME DOWN; GET UP; TAKE OUT

ACTIVITY 1: CONVERSATION PRACTICE

One friends calls another friend who is sick to see if he's feeling okay.

Read this conversation. Think about the meanings of the **3 new bold verbs**. Remember the meanings of the <u>underlined verbs</u> from earlier lessons. Then answer the comprehension questions.

Jacob: Hi, Kayla.

Kayla: Jacob! How are you? Amanda told me you weren't feeling so well, and I just wanted to see if you needed anything.

Jacob: I'm doing better, thanks. When I **got up** today, I felt a little better, but I don't feel 100%.

Kayla: What's wrong?

Jacob: I think I'm **coming down with** the flu. My body aches, and I'm just really tired.

Kayla: Well, are you taking anything?

Jacob: Yes, I took two aspirins this morning, and I may get back in bed now. I think I need to rest some more.

Kayla: That sounds like a smart idea.

Jacob: You're right. The only thing I tried to do today was to **take out** the garbage.

Kayla: I think you're right to take it as easy as you can.

Jacob: Well, I was going to <u>go out</u> and <u>pick up</u> a few things at the store, but I just didn't feel up to it, so I <u>came back</u> in the house. Then I just <u>ended up</u> lying on the sofa for a while.

Kayla: Well, Jacob, it doesn't sound like you were taking it easy at all.

Jacob: Yes, you're right.

Kayla: Have you tried to <u>set up</u> an appointment to see a doctor?

Jacob: No, I don't think it's that serious, not yet

anyway. I think I'm going to wait 24 hours and then see how I feel.

Kayla: Okay, but in the meantime, if you need anything, Jacob—anything at all—please let me know, okay?

Jacob: Yes, for sure. And I really appreciate your concern. I think I'm going to go back to sleep for a while.

Kayla: Okay, do that. I'll call you tomorrow again to see how you're doing.

1. Why did Kayla call Jacob?

   a. To invite him to go to the store.
   b. To check if he needed help.
   c. To ask him for his help.

2. What did Jacob do today?

   a. He went to see a doctor.
   b. He took out the garbage and went shopping.
   c. He took some medicine and rested.

3. What suggestion does Kayla give to Jacob?

   a. Take 2 aspirins and stay home.
   b. Rest and take it easy.
   c. Make an appointment to see a doctor immediately.

4. What is wrong with Jacob?

   a. He hurt himself when he was taking out the garbage.
   b. He feels bad because he did not pick up a few things at the store.
   c. He is coming down with something.

5. Which of these is true?

   a. Jacob's body hurts and he feels tired.
   b. Kayla thinks Jacob is taking it easy.
   c. Amanda told Kayla to call Jacob.

6. When did Jacob call the doctor's office?

   a. He hasn't called, but he may call tomorrow.
   b. He hasn't called, but he will call tomorrow.
   c. He is not going to call the doctor's office.

~

ACTIVITY 2: LEARNING NEW PHRASAL VERBS

Read this information about 3 phrasal verbs. Study the example sentences carefully. To help learn them, read the example sentences aloud or write them on a sheet of paper or in a document.

#25: COME DOWN

25A: move from a higher to a lower place

- I think the price of milk is **coming down.**
- In the storm last night, a lot of trees in our area **came down.**

25B: **COME DOWN TO**: ending with one thing as the most important part

- Success in anything often **comes down to** a lot of hard work.
- The match **came down to** penalty shots.

25C: **COME DOWN WITH**: become sick suddenly with an illness like a cold or the flu

- I think I'm **coming down with** the flu.
- Ben **came down with** a cold and couldn't work at the hospital today.

~

#26: GET UP

26A: wake up and leave bed

- My cat always **gets up** before I do.
- Most people set an alarm to **get up** on time.

26B: stand up

- I fell really hard and wasn't able to **get up** right away.
- We were sitting down, but when the bride entered, everyone **got up**.

∾

#27: TAKE OUT

27A: remove; withdraw

- Please don't forget to **take out** the garbage before you leave for work.
- I think I can use this card to **take out** some money from the bank.

27B: go to a restaurant, park, movie, etc., with someone you have invited

- I'm going to **take** my nephew **out** to the zoo next Saturday.
- Our boss **took** us **out** for lunch.

∾

ACTIVITY 3: PRACTICING IMPORTANT PHRASES

Give the phrasal verb for the meaning. Be sure to use the correct verb tense.

1. she got sick with a cold = she _____ _____ _____ a cold
2. a dentist can remove a tooth = a dentist can _____ _____ a tooth
3. the game was decided in the last minute = the game _____ _____ _____ the last minute
4. I invited them for lunch = I _____ them _____ for lunch
5. the opposite of *sit down* = _____ _____

~

ACTIVITY 4: USING CORRECT PREPOSITIONS

Read the sentences carefully and add the missing prepositions for each phrasal verb.

1. Okay, Jack, this is it. It all comes _____ _____ you. We need you to concentrate on this next shot.
2. If you've been sitting too long at your computer, you really should get _____ and stretch from time to time.
3. My front left tire had a nail in it, so I took it to a shop and they took _____ the nail and fixed the tire.
4. Just before their big trip, she came _____ _____ COVID and had to cancel everything.
5. My in-laws took us _____ for breakfast this morning.
6. The rain came _____ hard and flooded the street.

~

ACTIVITY 5: VERBS IN CONTEXT

Use the context to select the correct verb for the sentence.

1. I don't know if I can drive with you to Miami tomorrow. I think I might be (coming down, coming down to, coming down with, getting up, taking out) a cold.
2. If we have more restaurants, then the price of a meal out might (come down, come down to, come down with, get up, take out).
3. Don't (come down, come down to, get up, take out) your credit card until the light turns green.
4. How do you feel now? Do you think you can (come down to, come down with, get up, take out) and go for a walk with me?
5. The outcome of this election will (come down, come down to, come down with, get up, take out) how many people take part in the election.

～

ACTIVITY 6: ONLINE PRACTICE

You can practice the phrasal verbs from this lesson at

https://tinyurl.com/bdhvp2ek

Here you can use *Flashcards*, *Learn*, or *Match*. You can also have more guided practice with *Q-Chat*, which offers *Teach me*, *Quiz me*, and *Apply my knowledge*.

Answers for Lesson 9

Activity 1

1. b
2. c
3. b
4. c
5. a
6. a

Activity 3

1. came down with
2. take out
3. came down to
4. took ... out
5. get up

Activity 4

1. down to
2. up
3. out
4. down with
5. out
6. down

Activity 5

1. coming down with
2. come down
3. take out
4. get up
5. come down to

LESSON 10

SHOW UP; TAKE OFF; WORK OUT

ACTIVITY 1: CONVERSATION PRACTICE

Two friends are talking about an English class.

Read this conversation. Think about the meanings of the **3 new bold verbs**. Remember the meanings of the <u>underlined verbs</u> from earlier lessons. Then answer the comprehension questions.

Jennifer: Hey, how's your English class going?

David: So far, so good. I like the teacher and the other students a lot, and I really like the textbook we're using.

Jennifer: I'm glad to hear that, but I thought you said there was no class that matched your work schedule?

David: Yes, that was a problem at first, but then I talked to my boss, and we were able to **work out** something so I could go to class twice a week.

Jennifer: Wow, that's great that your boss was so helpful like that. What did you **work out**?

David: Well, on Monday and Wednesday he lets me **take off** early, and then I just <u>make up</u> those hours on Tuesday and Thursday.

Jennifer: Okay, so your Mondays and Wednesdays are shorter, which means your Tuesdays and Thursdays are longer, right?

David: Yes, that's what we **worked out**. So, on Tuesday and Thursday, I <u>get up</u> a lot earlier and start work at 7:30 instead of 9:00. I can still do all my work hours, and I get to go to my class, so it's a win-win.

Jennifer: How far is your class from where you work?

David: Well, that's a little bit of a problem. The class is really not so near where I work. If there's not a lot of traffic, then I can usually get there on time, but I have to leave work and get in my car right away.

Jennifer: Well, that's good to hear because I know traffic here in the city can be awful, especially in the afternoons when you're trying to drive to your class. Maybe you could use an app like Waze to help you <u>figure out</u> the shortest way to get to class on time.

David: You're absolutely right, and I use Waze already. Sometimes I do <u>end up</u> **showing up** a little late for class, though. But I've told my teacher about my job situation, and like I told you, she's just great and has been so wonderful about my schedule. I can usually get there on time, though.

Jennifer: That all sounds amazing. I'm so glad it all **worked out** for you.

David: Me, too. I really like that class.

1. How does David feel about his class?

    a. He likes the teacher and the students, but he does not like the book they use in class.
    b. He is very happy with everything.
    c. He prefers the morning class to the afternoon class.

2. On which of these days is David in English class?

    a. Tuesday
    b. Wednesday
    c. Thursday

3. How does David make up for the time he takes off from work for his class?

a. He works extra hours on the weekend.

b. He works longer hours on other days.

c. He doesn't need to make up the time.

4. What does David's teacher think about him coming to class late sometimes?

a. She has no problem with this situation.

b. She told him he can be late sometimes but not more than 15 minutes.

c. She thinks he should get a different job with a different work schedule.

5. What is Jennifer's overall reaction to David's situation?

a. She is worried because David has to drive a lot.

b. She is not satisfied with what David's boss did.

c. She is glad David can take the class.

6. Which of these is true?

a. Jennifer wants to be in the class with David.

b. David's boss was very helpful with the situation.

c. Mrs. Willis is a very strict teacher, but David likes her.

~

ACTIVITY 2: LEARNING NEW PHRASAL VERBS

Read this information about 3 phrasal verbs. Study the example sentences carefully. To help learn them, read the example sentences aloud or write them on a sheet of paper or in a document.

#28: SHOW UP

28A: appear at a public or social event

- Only five people **showed up** at today's meeting.
- If the pilot doesn't **show up**, they will have to cancel the flight.

28B: be visible or present

- A small fracture on my left arm **showed up** on the x-ray.
- I couldn't see the Northern Lights with my own eyes, but they **showed up** in a picture I took with my phone.

∿

#29: TAKE OFF

29A: remove

- In Japan, people **take off** their shoes before going into their house.

- It was hot in the room, so I **took off** my sweater.

29B: leave the ground

- Flight 652 **took off** on time.
- Many space rockets in the US **take off** from the east coast of Florida.

29C: leave a place suddenly

- The thief **took off** as soon as he heard the police car coming.
- As soon as my replacement showed up, I **took off** because it was after 5:00.

29D: become more successful

- Beyoncé's music career **took off** in 2003 with the release of her hit single "Crazy in Love."
- Sales of my book **took off** after some friends posted about it on social media.

∼

#30: WORK OUT

30A: happen successfully

- My new job is **working out** great.
- How did everything **work out**?

30B: solve

- If you call the help desk, they can help you **work out** your schedule.
- The teacher asked us to **work out** this problem and show our work on our paper.

30C: do certain physical activity to stay in better health

- You're in such good shape! How often do you **work out**?
- Do you think it's a little strange that some people drive four blocks to a gym to **work out**?

~

ACTIVITY 3: PRACTICING IMPORTANT PHRASES

Give the phrasal verb for the meaning. Be sure to use the correct verb tense.

1. appear at a meeting = _____ _____ at a meeting
2. his career became successful = his career _____ _____
3. airplanes leave the ground = airplanes _____ _____
4. exercise at the gym = _____ _____ at the gym
5. an error appeared in the bank report = an error _____ _____ in the bank report

~

ACTIVITY 4: USING CORRECT PREPOSITIONS

Read the sentences carefully and add the missing prepositions for each phrasal verb.

1. I was surprised that only a handful of people showed
   _____ at the meeting.
2. If the buyer can work _____ an agreement with the
   seller, then this deal may happen, but it all depends
   on how much the seller wants to sell this property
   right now.
3. Some say that Ed Sheeran's career really took _____
   with his song "A-Team" in 2011.
4. How many people showed _____ for the team
   meeting?
5. If we can work _____ these differences about teacher
   pay, I think we can have a new contract.
6. Our flight took _____ late because of bad weather in
   Chicago.

∽

ACTIVITY 5: VERBS IN CONTEXT

Use the context to select the correct verb for the sentence.

1. The song that really caused Madonna's career to
   (show up, take off, work out) in 1983 was "Holiday."
2. This business deal is complicated, but if everything
   (shows up, takes off, works out) well, we could make
   a lot of money.

3. My boss says she'll fire me if I (show up, take off, work out) late for work one more time.

4. In my opinion, not (showing up, taking off, working out) to work for a whole week without any good excuse is certainly a reason to be fired.

5. Our flight (showed up, took off, worked out) late, but we still arrived on time.

∾

ACTIVITY 6: ONLINE PRACTICE

You can practice the phrasal verbs from this lesson at

https://tinyurl.com/3d6h7p48

Here you can use *Flashcards, Learn,* or *Match.* You can also have more guided practice with *Q-Chat,* which offers *Teach me, Quiz me,* and *Apply my knowledge.*

Answers for Lesson 10

Activity 1

1. b
2. b
3. b
4. a
5. c
6. b

Activity 3

1. show up
2. took off
3. take off
4. work out
5. showed up

Activity 4

1. up
2. out
3. off
4. up
5. out
6. off

Activity 5

1. take off
2. works out
3. show up
4. showing up
5. took off

ACKNOWLEDGMENTS

Writing a book always entails multiple people, and I would like to thank those who helped make this book a reality. Thanks to my publisher at Wayzgoose, Dorothy Zemach, for her work on this series. Special thanks to my diligent content editor, Kelly Sippell, who used her special attention to detail to help keep me focused during the writing of this book. I am also grateful to the many people who helped me choose relevant and natural sounding examples for all these phrasal verbs, including James Currier, Ariel Bianchi, and Mary Goodman.

—Keith S. Folse

ABOUT THE AUTHOR

Dr. Keith S. Folse, Professor of TESOL (Teaching English to Speakers of Other Languages), University of Central Florida, teaches undergraduate, graduate, and doctoral classes. Originally secondary certified in English and French, he has taught English as a Second Language for 40 years in Saudi Arabia, Malaysia, Kuwait, Japan, Spain, and the United States. For the last eleven years, he has also taught online courses, both synchronously and asynchronously.

Dr. Folse is the author of 70 English and teacher education textbooks and is a frequent conference presenter all around the world. His presentations often deal with best teaching practices, vocabulary, grammar, and speaking. He has won numerous teaching and research awards from his university,

TESOL International Association, and National Geographic Learning.

ABOUT THE PUBLISHER

Thank you for your time and attention! If you found the book useful, we hope you will leave a short review on the site where you purchased this book to let other readers know of your experience.

To be notified about new titles and special contests, events, and sales from Wayzgoose Press, please visit our website at

http://wayzgoosepress.com

and sign up for our mailing list. (We send email infrequently, and you can unsubscribe at any time.)

~

www.ingramcontent.com/pod-product-compliance
Lightning Source LLC
Chambersburg PA
CBHW060812050426
42449CB00008B/1639